New Hampshire Wetlands and Waters:
Results of the National Wetlands Inventory

Ralph W. Tiner
U.S. Fish & Wildlife Service
National Wetlands Inventory Program
Northeast Region
300 Westgate Center Drive
Hadley, MA 01035

August 2007

This report should be cited as:

Tiner, R.W. 2007. New Hampshire Wetlands and Waters: Results of the National Wetlands Inventory. U.S. Fish and Wildlife Service, Northeast Region, Hadley, MA. NWI Technical Report. 21 pp.

Note: The findings and conclusions in the report are those of the author and do not necessarily represent the views of the U.S. Fish and Wildlife Service.

TABLE OF CONTENTS

INTRODUCTION

The U.S. Fish and Wildlife Service (FWS) has been conducting a nationwide survey of wetlands and deepwater habitats since the mid-1970s through its National Wetlands Inventory Program (NWI). This survey is accomplished using traditional photointerpretation techniques to produces map and digital geospatial data on the status of wetlands. The U.S. Geological Survey topographic maps serve as the base data upon which boundaries of wetlands and deepwater habitats are delineated. Wetlands are classified according to the FWS's official wetland classification system (Cowardin et al. 1979) which has been adopted as the national standard for reporting on the status and trends of U.S. wetlands by the Federal Geographic Data Committee (http://www.fws.gov/stand/standards/wetlands.txt).

Wetland mapping has been completed for over 90% of the coterminous U.S., all of Hawaii, and 35% of Alaska. For the Northeast, wetland mapping has been completed for 12 of the 13 states in the region; all but New York have been completely mapped. As time permits, the FWS summarizes the results of its NWI for geographic areas. Detailed state reports have been prepared for several states (Connecticut, Delaware, Maryland, and New Jersey), while data summary reports have been prepared for several other states in the northeastern United States: Massachusetts, Vermont, Pennsylvania, and West Virginia.

Wetland mapping for New Hampshire was completed in the 1990s and the data have been available online for several years. The data have not been summarized; this report provides a summary of the findings of the inventory.

Study Area

The state of New Hampshire encompasses 9,350 square miles in the northeastern United States. It ranks 46th among states in size and 41th in population as of 2005. The state contains 8,969 square miles of land and 382 square miles of water (http://infoplease.com).

From a natural landscape standpoint, the state falls within two of Bailey's ecoregions: Adirondack-New England Mixed Forest-Coniferous Forest-Alpine Meadow Province and Eastern Broadleaf Forest (Oceanic) Province (Bailey 1995). Due to its glacial history, the state contains numerous lakes and ponds with Lake Winnipesaukee being the largest (44,586 acres) and the most well-known. It is nearly seven times bigger than New Hampshire's next largest lake – Umbagog Lake (7,539 acres). Among the more prominent rivers are the Merrimack, Connecticut (forming nearly all of the state's western border with Vermont), Piscataqua (separating the southeastern part of the state from Maine), Saco, Androscoggin, and Ossipee. Politically, the state is divided into 10 counties (Figure 1, Table 1).

Figure 1. New Hampshire counties.

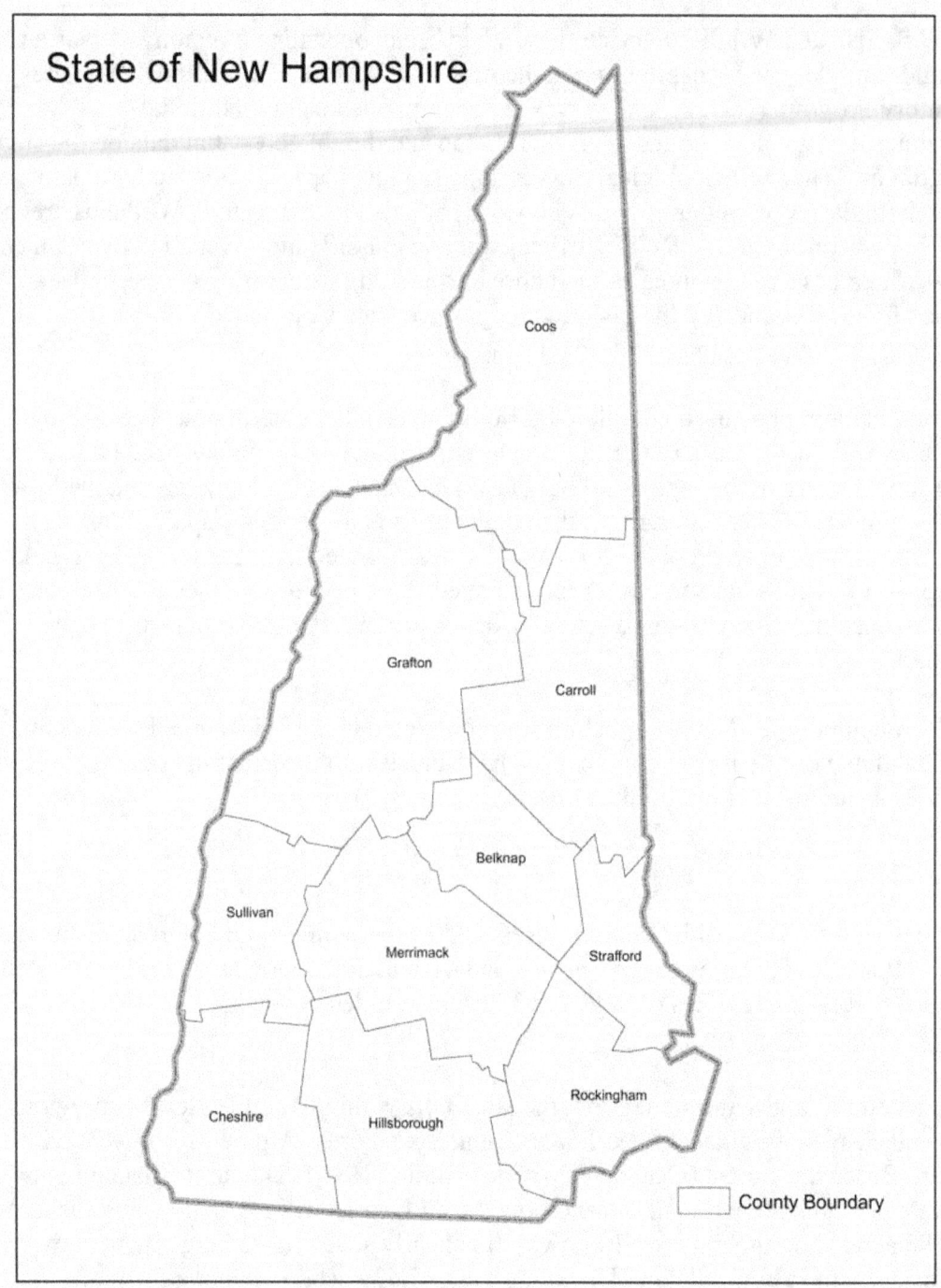

Table 1. New Hampshire counties and their land area in square miles.
(http://en.wikipedia.org)

County	Land Area (sq. miles)	Percent of State	Rank
Belknap	401	4.5	9
Carroll	934	10.4	4*
Cheshire	708	7.9	6
Coos	1801	20.1	1
Grafton	1714	19.1	2
Hillsborough	876	9.8	5
Merrimack	934	10.4	3*
Rockingham	695	7.7	7
Strafford	369	4.1	10
Sullivan	537	6.0	8
Total	8,969		

*According to the World Almanac and Book of Facts 1992, Merrimack County is slightly larger than Carroll County (936 sq. miles vs. 933 sq. miles), so the former is ranked number 3 in area.

METHODS

The NWI relies on photointerpretation of aerial photographs to locate and map wetlands and deepwater habitats. For New Hampshire, most of the aerial photography used was 1:58,000 color infrared captured from the spring of 1985 to the spring of 1987; a few state border quads have been updated with more recent imagery. With this imagery, the target mapping unit for wetlands ranges between 1-3 acres. This means that most wetlands larger than three acres should be mapped and that all wetlands are not mapped. Even with this target mapping unit established, it must be recognized that aerial photointerpretation has limitations in terms of the types of wetlands that can be readily identified (Tiner 1990, 1999) and that larger wetlands of certain types will escape detection and be missing from the maps. These limitations are generally outlined in Tables 1 and 2. The effective date of this inventory should be considered the mid-1980s.

Wetlands were classified according to the FWS's official wetland classification system (Cowardin et al. 1979). The following categories were identified for wetlands and deepwater habitats: system, subsystem, class, subclass, water regime, and a few special modifiers (e.g., partly drained, dike/impounded, excavated, and farmed). The organic soil modifier "g" was applied to Atlantic white cedar swamps (e.g., PFO4Bg) to highlight them; the acid modifier "a" was applied to bogs (e.g., PSS3Ba).

Wetland maps were prepared following standard NWI mapping conventions (U.S. Fish and Wildlife Service 1994, 1995). Data were digitized to create a geospatial database. NWI data are posted on the web at NWI home page: http://www.fws.gov/nwi/. Data were summarized by the NWI Mapping Support Center at Madison, Wisconsin. The following conventions were employed:

> 1. State and county boundaries were determined using the Geographic Data Technology's 1:100K states and counties layers. These were used due to the lack of a consistent nationwide layer of boundaries at the 1:24,000 scale.

> 2. All marine deepwater habitats (M1___) were removed from the analysis. The decision to remove them from the analysis was made due to the lack of validity of this acreage value. The marine system extends far beyond the mapped area and is ended at 1:250K quad boundaries rendering the acreage meaningless.

> 3. Areas where county or state boundaries consisted of two-line waterbodies, (i.e. rivers, streams) the boundary was identified and digitized directly from a USGS 1:24,000 DRG.

The data was summarized by county and aggregated by state in two categories: 1) system, subsystem, class, and subclass and 2) system and water regime. Any differences in state and county totals are due to round-off procedures.

Table 1. Major NWI map limitations. (Adapted from Tiner 1999.)

1. Target mapping unit – minimum size wetland that NWI is attempting to map which is generally related to the scale of the imagery: 1-3 acres for 1:58,000 photography.

2. Spring photography – aquatic beds and nonpersistent emergent wetlands may be undermapped since these types are usually obscured by high water. In some cases, flooded emergents may be misclassified as scrub-shrub wetlands.

3. Forested wetlands – forested wetlands on glacial till are difficult to photointerpret as are temporarily flooded or seasonally saturated types, especially on the coastal plain and on glaciolacustrine plains; they may be under-represented by the existing NWI mapping. *Such areas may be identified by examining U.S. Department of Agriculture soil survey maps for hydric soil map units that are undeveloped (i.e., areas of undeveloped hydric soil map units that were not mapped by NWI represent areas that may contain wetlands).*

4. Estuarine and tidal waters – delineation of the break between estuarine and riverine (tidal) systems should be considered approximate.

5. Tidal flats – since imagery was not tide synchronized, tidal flat boundaries were based on aerial photointerpretation in consultation with collateral data such as U.S. Geological Survey topographic maps.

6. Coastal wetlands – identification of high marsh (irregularly flooded) vs. low marsh (regularly flooded) in tidal marshes is conservative; photo-signatures are not distinctive in many instances.

7. Water regimes – water regime classification is based on photo-signatures coupled with limited field verification; they should be considered approximate.

8. Linear wetlands (long, narrow) – they follow drainageways and stream corridors and may or may not be mapped depending on project objectives. Most NWI maps identify at least some of these features, but no attempt was made to map all of them.

9. Partly drained wetlands – they are conservatively mapped; many are not shown on NWI maps.

10. Aerial photography – imagery reflects wetness during the specific year and season it was acquired.

11. Drier-end wetlands (temporarily flooded and seasonally saturated types) – they are difficult to photointerpret; many have been mapped by consulting hydric soil data from the U.S.D.A. Natural Resources Conservation Service.

12. Mapped boundaries – they may be somewhat different than if based on detailed field observations, especially in areas with subtle changes in topography.

Table 2. Specific problems noted during photointerpretation of New Hampshire wetlands.

1. High tide and ice-scouring obscured low marsh (E2EM1N) areas along the Merrimack River. The "Soil Survey of New Hampshire Tidal Marshes" (USDA Soil Conservation Service 1974) was used to help identify lower limits of salt marshes. This survey plus field checking were used to help make salt-fresh (Estuarine-Riverine tidal) breaks.

2. Forested wetlands were difficult to identify on some images due to indistinct signatures or to leaf-out (e.g., May 1986 photos were particularly problematic also for separating evergreen from deciduous forested wetlands). Soil survey information and USGS swamp symbols and contours were used to help separate the wet forests from the upland forests. Mapping of forested wetlands is conservative.

3. E1UB4L was used to classify salt marsh pannes greater than 3 acres in size.

4. Mixed palustrine emergent and scrub-shrub wetlands may underestimate the amount of shrubby vegetation due to photo-signature.

5. 1986 photos showed a lot more water than appeared on the USGS topographic map and seemed to have higher water levels than the 1985 photos for neighboring areas.

6. March 1985 photos had some ice on ponds and lakes making classification difficult; snow on land areas presented similar classification problems. Additional field work in subject areas was performed to resolve these issues as much as time/budget would permit.

7. Presence of dams on the Connecticut River caused river to be classified as L1UBHh far upstream due to impoundment effect. Intermittently flooded channels associated with dams along the Connecticut River were classified as R4 (Riverine Intermittent) habitat.

8. Sewage treatment ponds were classified with "K" (artificial) water regime.

9. Timber harvest (including slash piles) created dark signatures resembling wetland signature; limited delineations to low areas (depressions).

10. One photo has significant cloud cover requiring interpreters to consult adjacent photos (overlapping images) to identify wetlands.

11. There may be significant seepage wetlands in mountainous areas as interpreters noted swamp symbols on USGS topographic maps extending upslope 4-8 contours. Photointerpreters relied on photo-signatures and soil surveys for inaccessible sites to aid in mapping which probably led to conservative mapping of these wetland types. USGS 15-minute topographic maps tended to have extensive wetlands via symbology, but interpreters relied more on photo-signatures as they felt that much of those areas looked like dry forests at least from a signature standpoint.

12. Interpretation of wetlands along the Merrimack River were difficult due to imagery; USDA soil survey was used to help identify wetlands and classify their water regime.

RESULTS

Wetland Maps

NWI maps for New Hampshire were prepared in the 1990s, except for some state border quads that were done as parts of NWI work in adjacent states. These maps were produced at a scale of 1:24,000 using the U.S. Geological Survey topographic maps as base maps. Hardcopy maps are available for purchase through the Office of State Planning, State of New Hampshire, 2 ½ Beacon Street, Concord, NH 03301 (Attn: Bea Jillette; 603-271-2155).

After publication of the hardcopy maps, the NWI maps were converted to digital form for computer access and geographic information system (GIS) applications. Since the 1990s, the NWI Program has stopped production of hardcopy maps, replacing them with digital wetland geospatial data. All NWI data are now available online at the NWI website: http://www.fws.gov/nwi/. Some maps along state lines may have been updated since the original maps were produced and are available only online. To access NWI data, visit the NWI website, click on the "Wetlands Mapper", then click on the map of the lower 48 states, and finally zoom into the location of interest to see the wetland data for a specific area. Digital NWI data can also be downloaded for GIS use at this website. Digital NWI data are also available through the state GIS website: http://www.granit.sr.unh.edu/ but check to make sure that the latest data are posted at this site.

A map showing the distribution of New Hampshire's wetlands and waters is provided as Figure 2. This is a reduction of the original map which was produced at a scale of 1:275,000.

Figure 2. Map showing the distribution of wetlands and waters of New Hampshire excluding marine offshore waters. (Note: This is a reduced version of original figure.)

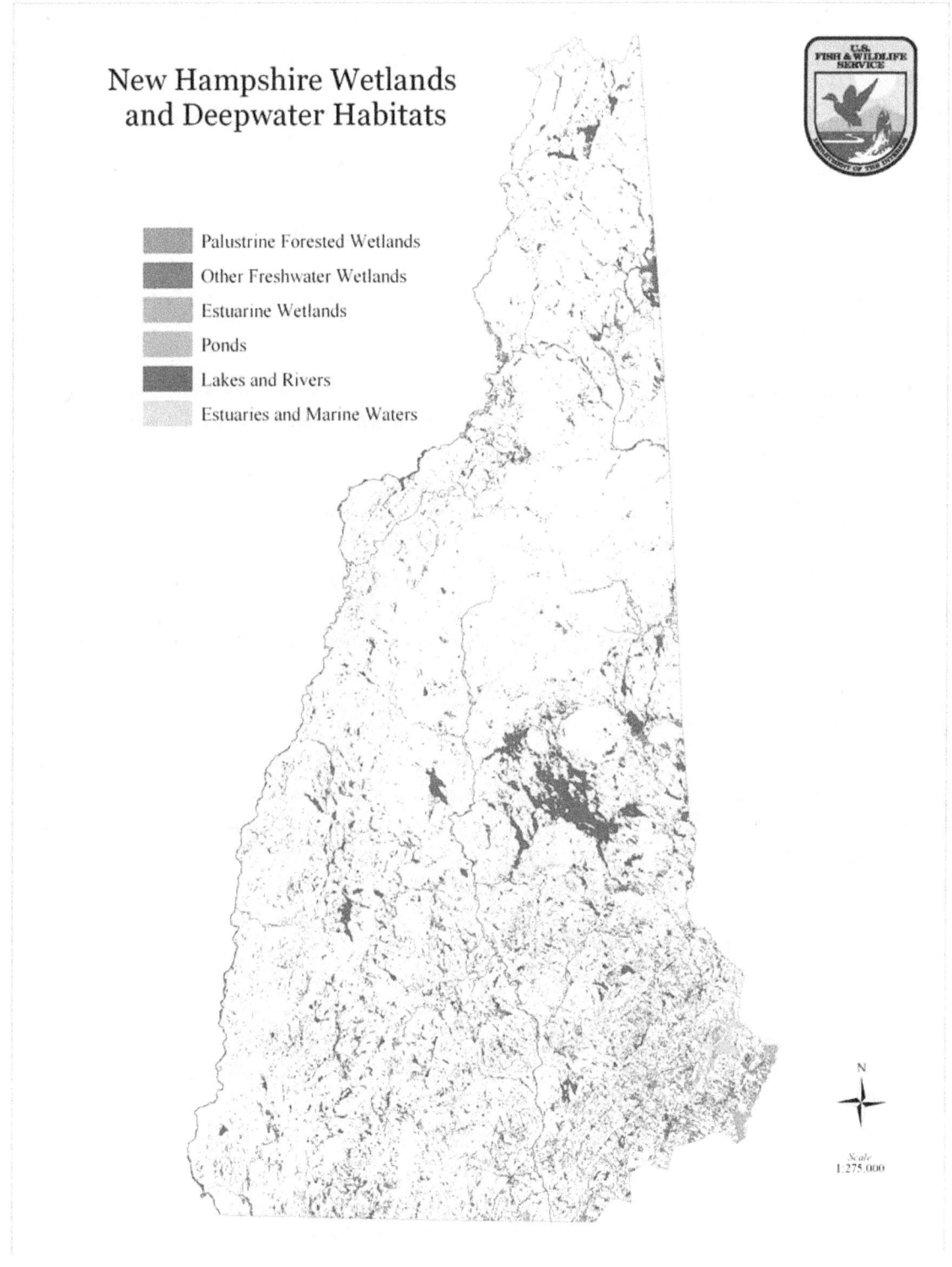

State Totals

Wetlands. The NWI identified nearly 290,000 acres of wetlands, covering 5% of the state's land area (Table 3). Palustrine wetlands are the main type, totaling about 278,000 acres and representing 96% of the state's wetland area. Fifty percent of the palustrine wetlands (or 48% of all wetlands) were forested types, with scrub-shrub wetlands making up slightly more than one-quarter (26%) of the freshwater wetlands, emergent wetlands representing 14% of these wetlands, and ponds (unconsolidated bottom and shores) account for nearly 9%.

Only 8,029 acres of estuarine wetlands occur, occupying nearly 3% of the wetland area. Emergent wetlands (salt and brackish marshes) were the most common estuarine wetlands, accounting for 70% of the estuarine wetlands. Unconsolidated shores (tidal flats) made up 29% of the estuarine wetlands.

Riverine, lacustrine, and marine wetlands when combined account for 2,792 acres which is roughly 1% of the state's wetlands. Riverine unconsolidated shores represented most of this acreage (1,447 acres).

Deepwater Habitats. Approximately 204,000 acres of deepwater habitats were inventoried, excluding marine waters and waters of linear streams. Lacustrine waters accounted for 82% of the state's water area (166,777 acres). Riverine waters were next in area with 20,260 acres mapped (15 tidal acres, 18,440 lower perennial acres, 1,803 acres upper perennial acres, and 15 acres of undetermined perennial), followed by 17,087 acres of estuarine waters.

County Totals

Wetlands. The acreage of wetlands by type is given for each county in Table 4. Rockingham County had the most wetland acreage with about 61,000 acres inventoried. Four other counties had over 30,000 acres: Coos, Hillsborough, and Merrimack. The wetlands in these counties accounted for almost 60% of the state wetlands.   The highest density of wetlands was found in Rockingham County with nearly 14% of its land area occupied by wetlands (Table 5). Strafford County was next ranked in wetland density with slightly more than 8% of its land area represented by wetland.

Deepwater Habitats. Belknap County had the highest acreage of deepwater habitat, followed closely by Carroll County (Table 6). Lake Winnipesaukee, New Hampshire's largest lake, was responsible for the predominance of deepwater habitat in these counties. Belknap County had, by far, the highest proportion of its area occupied by deepwater habitat – nearly 17%. Strafford and Carroll Counties each had about 6% of their area covered by deep water. Estuarine waters were nearly equally abundant in Rockingham and Strafford Counties where they represented a half or more of the deepwater habitats.

Table 3. Wetland acreage summaries for the state of New Hampshire. State totals differ from sum of county totals due to round-off procedures.

Ecological System	Wetland Class	Acreage
Marine	Aquatic Bed	254
	----------------------------	------
	Subtotal Vegetated	254
	Rocky Shore	18
	Unconsolidated Shore	363
	----------------------------	------
	Subtotal Nonvegetated	381
	Total Marine	*635*
Estuarine	Aquatic Bed	137
	Emergent	5,584
	----------------------------	----------
	Subtotal Vegetated	5,721
	Unconsolidated Shore	2,308
	----------------------------	--------
	Subtotal Nonvegetated	2,308
	Total Estuarine	*8,029*
Palustrine	Aquatic Bed	199
	Emergent	38,719
	Forested	139,401
	Scrub-Shrub	73,506
	----------------------------	-------------
	Subtotal Vegetated	251,825
	Unconsolidated Bottom	26,059
	Unconsolidated Shore	55
	----------------------------	-------------
	Subtotal Nonvegetated	26,114
	Total Palustrine	*277,939*

Table 3. Continued

Lacustrine	Aquatic Bed	85
	Emergent (nonpersistent)	111
	Subtotal Vegetated	196
	Unconsolidated Bottom	170
	Unconsolidated Shore	302
	Subtotal Nonvegetated	472
	Total Lacustrine	*668*
Riverine	Unconsolidated Shore	1,447
	Rocky Shore	6
	Streambed	36
	Subtotal Nonvegetated	1,489
	Total Riverine	*1,489*
ALL WETLANDS		**288,760**

Table 4. NWI findings for each county. Numbers represent acres of wetlands.

NWI Type	Belknap	Carroll	Cheshire	Coos	Grafton	Hillsborough
Palustrine Wetlands						
Aquatic Bed	5	11	--	51	36	28
Emergent	2,319	2,971	3,651	3,275	3,115	7,125
Forested	5,154	16,842	10,610	20,068	8,744	15,864
Scrub-Shrub	3,043	6,369	7,124	14,358	6,225	8,999
Unconsol. Bottom	1,505	1,800	2,564	1,879	2,664	4,598
Lacustrine Wetlands						
Aquatic Bed	--	--	--	--	--	42
Emergent	--	--	25	24	29	--
Unconsolidated. Shore	2	--	5	251	14	13
Unconsolidated Bottom	--	--	--	--	1	86
Riverine Wetlands						
Unconsol. Shore	2	350	37	220	681	34
Rocky Shore	2	--	--	--	1	--
Streambed	--	--	20	3	10	--
Total	12,032	28,343	24,036	40,129	21,520	36,789

13

Table 4 (continued).

NWI Type	Merrimack	Rockingham	Strafford	Sullivan
Palustrine Wetlands				
Aquatic Bed	1	30	--	38
Emergent	5,359	6,677	2,402	1,826
Forested	14,222	32,531	11,040	4,326
Scrub-Shrub	9,706	10,038	4,031	3,615
Unconsol. Bottom	4,267	3,816	1,613	1,407
Lacustrine Wetlands				
Aquatic Bed	--	43	--	--
Emergent	--	--	33	--
Unconsolidated. Shore	2	1	--	15
Unconsolidated Bottom	40	25	--	18
Riverine Wetlands				
Unconsol. Shore	48	--	1	74
Rocky Shore	2	--	--	--
Streambed	3	--	--	--
Estuarine Wetlands				
Aquatic Bed	--	134	3	--
Emergent	--	5,369	215	--
Unconsol. Shore	--	1,864	444	--
Marine Wetlands				
Aquatic Bed	--	254	--	--
Unconsol. Shore	--	363	--	--
Rocky Shore	--	18	--	--
Total	33,650	61,163	19,782	11,319

County

14

Table 5. Ranking of counties by wetland area. Percent of county comprised by wetlands is also given.

Rank	County	Wetland Acreage	Percent of County Land Area
1	Rockingham	61,163	13.8
2	Coos	40,129	3.5
3	Hillsborough	36,789	6.6
4	Merrimack	33,650	5.6
5	Carroll	28,343	4.7
6	Cheshire	24,036	5.3
7	Grafton	21,520	2.0
8	Strafford	19,782	8.4
9	Belknap	12,032	4.7
10	Sullivan	11,319	3.3

Table 6. Acreage of deepwater habitats in New Hampshire counties. Riverine waters are separated into lower perennial, upper perennial, and tidal types. Percent of county occupied by deepwater habitats (both excluding and including marine waters) is given and rank by acreage.

County	Lacustrine Waters	Riverine Waters			Estuarine Waters	Total Waters	% of of Co.	(Rank)
		Lower	Upper	Tidal				
Belknap	42,815	376	13	--	--	43,204	16.8	(1)
Carroll	37,012	747	151	--	--	37,910	6.3	(2)
Cheshire	10,290	2,364	125	--	--	12,779	2.8	(8)
Coos	16,664	3,163	156	--	--	19,983	1.7	(4)
Grafton	18,402	4,142	595	--	--	23,139	2.1	(3)
Hillsborough	7,680	2,113	149	--	--	9,942	1.8	(9)
Merrimack	11,200	2,902	349	--	--	14,451	2.4	(7)
Rockingham	9,717	139	40	2	8,832	18,730	4.2	(5)
Strafford	6,359	291	128	13	8,255	15,046	6.4	(6)
Sullivan	6,639	2,202	99	--	--	8,940	2.6	(10)

DISCUSSION

Comparison with Hydric Soil Acreage

The U.S.D.A. National Resources Conservation Service has conducted soil surveys for New Hampshire during which soil scientists have identified wet soils that are now called "hydric soils." Over 50 soil series and land types representing potential wetlands have been mapped since the 1930s (Table 7). While these areas are dominated by hydric soils (e.g., poorly drained and very poorly drained soils), even soil map units of better drained soils have some hydric soil as inclusions.

According to the latest soil survey statistics, over 576,000 acres of hydric soils have been mapped in New Hampshire: 41,112 acres of hydric Entisols (e.g., floodplain soils), 152,119 acres of Histosols (organic soils: peats and mucks), 43,767 acres of Spodosols (evergreen forest soils), and 339,388 acres of Inceptisols (other mostly forest soils) (Paul Finnell, USDA NRCS, National Soils Database Manager, pers. comm. 2007). When compared with the wetlands mapped by NWI, we find a considerable difference in the acreage in New Hampshire that may be covered by wetlands: 290,000 acres (NWI) vs. 576,000 acres (soil surveys). There are, however, several reasons for the differences including: 1) more generalized mapping of soils (e.g., larger map units) than the more detailed mapping of wetlands by NWI, 2) the different dates of the soil surveys vs. NWI (changes likely have taken place in the presence of wetlands since the original soil survey), and 3) difficulty in photointerpreting the drier-end wetlands, especially seasonally saturated forested wetlands (results in conservative mapping by NWI; such areas are likely shown as hydric soil mapping units on the soil surveys). Overall, the NWI estimates are conservative due to the limitations in the ability to photointerpret wetlands (see discussion in Methods), while the soil survey numbers are probably liberal due to their age and mapping techniques (e.g., minimum mapping sizes and interpretation of large forest tracts). The conclusion is that the actual extent of wetlands probably lies somewhere between the two numbers. From the statewide perspective, then, the acreage of wetlands ranges between 290,000 acres (NWI) and 576,386 acres. Consequently wetlands may occupy anywhere between 5-10 percent of the state.

Table 7. List of hydric soil series and some land types associated with New Hampshire's wetlands based on soil survey mapping since the 1930s. (Note: List may not be complete.)

Alluvial Land, Mixed, Wet	Alluvial Land, Wet
Bemis	Biddeford
Binghamville	Borohemists
Bucksport	Burnham
Cabot	Charles
Chocorua	Cohas
Endoaquents	Grange
Greenwood	Fresh Water Marsh
Ipswich	Kinsman
Leicester (and variant)	Lim
Limerick (and variant)	Lyme
Maybid	Medomak
Monarda	Moosilauke
Muck and Peat	Naumburg
Ossipee	Pawcatuck
Peacham	Pemi
Pillsbury	Pipestone
Pondicherry	Raynham (and variant)
Ridgebury	Rippowam
Roundabout	Rumney
Saco (and variant)	Saugatuck
Scantic	Scarboro
Scitico	Searsport
Squamscott	Stissing
Swanton	Tidal Marsh
Vassalboro	Walpole
Wareham	Westbrook
Whitman	Wonsqueak

CONCLUSION

The NWI Program mapped about 290,000 acres of wetlands and over 200,000 acres of deepwater habitats, excluding marine waters, for the state. The wetland mapping is conservative due to limitations of the photointerpretation techniques employed. Considering NRCS hydric soil data, the actual extent of wetlands in New Hampshire is likely somewhere between 290,000 and 576,000 acres, representing 5-10% of the state's land area.

ACKNOWLEDGMENTS

Numerous individuals contributed to the mapping of New Hampshire's wetlands. Wetland photointerpretation was performed by staff at the University of Massachusetts, Forestry and Wildlife Department: by David Foulis, Robert Popp, George Springston, David Sumpter, Kim Santos, Michael Kowal, Janice Stone, Glenn Smith, Catherine Cornell, Tim Moore, Anthony Davis, Gail Shaughnessy, John Organ, Judy Harding, and Frank Shumway. John Anderson (formerly U.S. Fish & Wildlife Service) also interpreted a few areas. Ralph Tiner coordinated the inventory for the U.S. Fish and Wildlife Service (FWS).

Ralph Tiner, John Organ, Bill Zinni, and Glenn Smith (FWS) were responsible for providing regional quality control of the inventory products during various stages of this project. Cartographic work was performed under the direction of the FWS's National Wetlands Inventory Center, St. Petersburg, Florida. GIS analysis of the data for this report was done by Mitch Bergeson (U.S. Geological Survey) working for the NWI Mapping Support Center at Madison, Wisconsin.

Paul R. Finnell, USDA Natural Resources Conservation Service, National Soil Survey Center, Lincoln, Nebraska provided the summary of hydric soil data for New Hampshire referenced in this report. Eric Derleth (FWS, New England Field Office) offered his photograph of the Thompson Sanctuary wetlands (North Sandwich) for use as the cover for this report.

REFERENCES

Bailey, R.G. 1995. Description of the Ecoregions of the United States. U.S.D.A. Forest Service, Washington, DC. http://www.fs.fed.us/land/ecosysmgmt/ecoreg1_home.html

Cowardin, L.M., V. Carter, F.C. Golet, and E.T. LaRoe. 1979. Classification of Wetlands and Deepwater Habitats of the United States. U.S. Fish and Wildlife Service, Washington, DC. FWS/OBS-79/31.

Tiner, R.W., Jr. 1990. Use of high-altitude aerial photography for inventorying forested wetlands in the United States. For. Ecol. Manage. 33/34: 593-604.

Tiner, R.W. 1999. Wetland Indicators: A Guide to Wetland Identification, Delineation, Classification, and Mapping. Lewis Publishers, CRC Press, Boca Raton, FL.

U.S. D.A. Soil Conservation Service. 1974. Soil Survey of New Hampshire Tidal Marshes. Durham, NH.

U.S. Fish and Wildlife Service. 1995. Photo Interpretation Conventions for the National Wetlands Inventory. NWI Project, St. Petersburg, FL.

U.S. Fish and Wildlife Service. 1994. Cartographic Conventions for the National Wetlands Inventory. NWI Project, St. Petersburg, FL.

U.S. Department of the Interior
Fish and Wildlife Service

http://www.fws.gov

September 2007